At the Restaurant

by Kyle Wagner
illustrated by Brandon Reese

Harcourt
SCHOOL PUBLISHERS

Printed in China

ISBN 10: 0-15-351505-8
ISBN 13: 978-0-15-351505-7

Ordering Options
ISBN 10: 0-15-351213-X (Grade 3 Advanced Collection)
ISBN 13: 978-0-15-351213-1 (Grade 3 Advanced Collection)
ISBN 10: 0-15-358095-X (package of 5)
ISBN 13: 978-0-15-358095-6 (package of 5)

3 4 5 6 7 8 9 10 985 12 11 10 09 08

Characters

Caitlin	**Claudia**	**Lisa**
Ken	**Adam**	**George**

Setting: The dining room of a restaurant

Caitlin: Today we're reporting from the main dining room of the Ivy Café, one of Springfield's most popular restaurants.

Adam: We're happy to be talking to Lisa O'Connell, the owner and head chef, as well as some of her staff. We're hoping they'll give us information about running a restaurant. There must be a lot to do every day, Lisa!

Lisa: There sure is, but if you're busy in a restaurant, that means things are going well!

Caitlin: Lisa, why don't you tell us about how you got started?

Lisa: I always loved to cook. I constantly experimented in the kitchen when I was your age. Some things turned out great. Some didn't. My parents sat through some really awful dinners I ruined! Still, they encouraged me to keep trying.

Adam: That must have made you feel good.

Lisa: It gave me confidence. I needed that when I went to cooking school and started to work in restaurants. There are many talented chefs out there. It's very competitive.

Caitlin: What made you decide to open your own place?

Lisa: I worked in many restaurants, but I always talked about my own ideas. Finally, a friend suggested that I open my own place and try them out!

Adam: Is it different being the owner?

Lisa: It's an enormous burden. You don't just cook. You have to decide everything from the restaurant's hours to the color of the napkins. I love it, though. It's a glorious feeling when you see the delighted looks on your customers' faces.

Caitlin: What's a day at the restaurant like for you?

Lisa: We're only open for dinner, but my day still starts early. I like to use fresh, locally-grown ingredients in my recipes, so I go to the farmer's market first. I buy what looks good and begin to get ideas about what I'll cook that day.

Adam: Do you really come up with new recipes every day?

Lisa: Yes. Some dishes are always on the menu, but then I add special items.

Caitlin: Do you cook everything yourself?

Lisa: Oh, no! I couldn't. I have many helpers in the kitchen. Everyone has an important job to do. Some cook meat. Some help make sauces. Some chop vegetables. Some clean up and wash the dishes.

Adam: You must do a lot in advance.

Lisa: We do as much as we can. We want everyone's food to be freshly made, but the customers can't wait hours for it. We can do some things, such as prepare vegetables for salad or clean fish, in the afternoon. Claudia, our pastry chef also gets a head start.

Caitlin: Claudia, can you tell us about what you do?

Claudia: Sure. A pastry chef makes desserts.

Adam: You must be very popular!

Claudia: I hope so! As Lisa said, I start early. Desserts usually don't cook quickly. Cakes and pies need time to bake. Ice cream needs time to chill.

Caitlin: How do you decide what to make?

Claudia: I go to the farmer's market for inspiration, too. I like to use fruit in my desserts, so it often depends on what is ripe and looks good.

Adam: New dinner items and new desserts every night must mean that the servers and buspersons have to learn something new every day.

Lisa: They do. They have a hard job!

Caitlin: How do they learn everything?

Lisa: I have a trick—I make them a nice dinner where we sit together and talk about that night's menu! Being there for the staff dinner is mandatory, but we try to make it fun.

Adam: Ken, you're one of the servers here. How do you get ready for the dinner customers?

Ken: Well, I listen carefully to everything Lisa says.

Lisa: I'm glad to hear that!

Ken: We also get written versions of the menu items. I immerse myself in that list and rehearse until I know everything by heart. I want to know everything about each menu item in case customers have questions. It's important to sound confident and knowledgeable when you have a dialogue with a customer.

Caitlin: What's it like when the restaurant opens?

Ken: It can get crazy! You have to take orders at your tables and bring the orders to the kitchen. Then you need to make sure all your other customers are happy. You ask them if they like their food, and you see if they need anything else. Then you may have to rush back and deliver another table's food. You have to juggle a lot of tasks.

Adam: How do you stay calm?

Lisa: George helps a lot. Why don't you tell about your job, George?

George: I'm the host. I'm the first person customers meet when they come in the door. I check and see whether or not there's a table ready. If there isn't, I try to tell them how long the wait will be. I give them menus to study, and I try to make them feel welcome. I keep an eye on the servers and buspersons, too. If someone is really busy, I can deliver food or check on the customers.

Lisa: George always keeps everything running smoothly. His efforts are heroic.

Caitlin: It sounds like everyone really has to work together.

Lisa: Absolutely! It's like being part of a great team.

Adam: Is that the best part of working in a restaurant?

Lisa: It's one of them. The other is seeing your customers have a good time.

Caitlin: What's the hardest part?

Lisa: Well, you know that people are going to criticize your work. If people do complain, you have to treat them in a tender way. It's important to listen to criticism. You might learn something important.

Adam: Lisa, what would you tell someone who wants to be in the restaurant business?

Lisa: I'd say that people interested in the restaurant business should try lots of different foods. Learn about what you like. Look at recipes, and study how cooking works. Also, go to restaurants, and think about what makes that restaurant a fun place. Most importantly, be ready to be busy! It's a fun business, but it's a lot of work!

Caitlin: That's great advice! Thanks, everybody!

Lisa: Come back for dinner!

Think Critically

1. How is preparing vegetables like being a pastry chef? How is it different?
2. What is the theme of this Readers' Theater?
3. What do you think the hardest part of a server's job is?
4. Who meets customers when they first arrive at the restaurant?
5. Which job in a restaurant would you like to have? Explain your choice.

Drama

Play Restaurant Write another scene that might take place after this restaurant opens for dinner. Ask classmates to help read it aloud.

School-Home Connection Ask a family member to cook something with you. Work together to choose a recipe, get the ingredients, prepare the dish, and then clean up.

Word Count: 1,057